She's Beyond
Those Thoughts

She's Beyond Those Thoughts

A personal conversation and guide for
women on positive thinking & success . . .

Tameisha Davis

authorHOUSE®

AuthorHouse™ LLC
1663 Liberty Drive
Bloomington, IN 47403
www.authorhouse.com
Phone: 1-800-839-8640

Published by AuthorHouse 01/16/2014

ISBN: 978-1-4918-5177-7 (sc)
ISBN: 978-1-4918-5176-0 (hc)
ISBN: 978-1-4918-5175-3 (e)

Library of Congress Control Number: 2014901126

 Contents

Special Acknowledgements ix

Preface.. xi

Introduction.. xiii

Defining that defining moment 3

Finding you in the process 17

A passion for passion 31

Got that covered 47

Finally out of the box 61

It's a MIND thing..73

Playback Exercises 85

About The Author 93

A special dedication to my two sons,

Keenen & Kelden. I love you more than you will ever know.

I am blessed to have you. And to my friend Kelly,
thank you for your love and support. I want to thank
you all for gracing my life with your presence.

I LOVE YOU!!!!

Special Acknowledgements

First and foremost, I would like to thank the DIVINE, higher power, ruler of the universe, the almighty God, for continuous blessings, wisdom, guidance, learning and knowledge on this path and journey in my life. I am beyond the words to describe the blessings. Next, I want to take this opportunity to give special thanks to some fantastic women whom I have been blessed to have in my life. To my loving and caring mom (Valeria Davis), I send a special thank you for being that light in a dark tunnel, and my support system. To my sweet sister (Catherine Davis), thank you for being my best friend, and confidant. To my wise grandmothers (Eula, Pearl) & late (Lula, Ora-Lee), thank you for instilling in me morals, values, and ethics. To aunts, cousins, and friends thank you for your personal examples which helped in the writing of this book. To a special teacher (Ivy Cobbins), thank you for opening up my world to a whole new experience. To all the women who affected my life in one way or another, I thank you, and I LOVE YOU. Ladies, this one is for you. Lastly, I would like to say thank you to everyone who lend me a helping hand, kind word, advice, feedback, and response in the writing of this book. It is greatly appreciated. Thank you, thank you, and thank you all.

Preface

Ladies, have you ever wondered and asked yourself, "is this as good as life gets?" I am sure many of us have. I will speak for most of us when I say that we have. We all would love to live like they do in the movies or at least like those famous people on television. They seem so happy, carefree, having fun and in utter bliss. However, in the "real" world, life doesn't always permit this. As regular people going about our daily lives, and trying to make ends meet, that sort of life is completely unrealistic. Who has the time, and money to be having fun, right? People have bills to pay, and families to feed. No one has time to live in fairy tale land. This is the real world. This is the land of leaving dreams and imagination in your childhood. The land of get up and go to work every day to earn a living. The land of when you reach adult age, leave the nest, go out and stand on your own two feet. The land of you have to do what you have to do to survive. The land of trying to make it from one day to the next. It's a cruel land. Cruel world!

What if there was a way to live the "famous" life. Would you want to? Would you be willing to? Besides, I don't know about you but I want to live like a superstar, LOL. I have a surprise for you. Guess what! Guess what! There is actually a way that we can live the life we dream of. How, you ask? Positive thinking! Yes, I said positive thinking. Well, isn't that a surprise, you don't have to settle for a routine, mundane and a boring life? The power of positive thinking can help us achieve the life that we want. All we have to do is tap into that power and watch our lives transform.

To all reading this guide, you may be thinking, "oh no, not another self-help book" well you may be correct, but this isn't just any self-help book. This is a guide to help women learn how to think positive and achieve a life of success and happiness. When I speak of both success and happiness they have different meanings and varies from person to person and from situation to situation. Therefore, when I talk about how to achieve success, in fact I am referring to something that fills a person with a sense of purpose, and fulfillment. I want to inspire, and encourage women to tap into their potential of greatness using positive thoughts. Additionally, I want my fellow ladies to understand that we do not have to give into this notion of mediocrity, routine and boredom. Together we can stand strong in the fight against the shackles of boredom, and mediocrity. Women! The power that we possess is simply amazing, and I am here to let you know that we must utilize our powers (Positive Thoughts) in a way that will help to transform this world. Let us transcend to higher heights, move mountains, maneuver obstacles, knocked down walls, break glass ceilings, and expand our horizons. Let us live happily with an abundance of love, success, joy, excitement and fulfillment. I want every lady reading this book and even if you are not a lady to be empowered, inspired, motivated and uplifted. It is here I will share some of my wisdom and knowledge in an effort to help you do so. I believe this is important for continuous growth, so help me to help you.

Introduction

When I have a problem, the first thing I do is call my girlfriend. So, when I decided to take on the task of writing this book I didn't want it to be seen as another self-help book or guide. I want you to think of me as your girlfriend and this book as our conversation. It's just you and I engaged in one on one, chit chat, girl talk that will ultimately create dialogue, form connections, initiate expressions, and allow healing. This is where we will address our most intimate feelings, thoughts, desires wants and needs that will help change the lives of many women. Let us get close and personal in our conversation here, as well. This guide is real, raw, honest, thought-provoking, unique, different, humorous yet serious at the same time. Just like what you would experience with me in an actual personal encounter. I'M GONNA BE ME. So either you like me or you will not. However, I am hoping by the end of our conversation you would consider me your friend. Let me start by saying that I am not your average lady. I am going to say some things, and speak in a way that you may or may not have heard them before. I promise to get a little loud and aggressive when I need to make a point. I promise to threaten, and talk rude to you but in a loving kind of way. I even promise to throw in a curse word or two. I promise to get sarcastic, scolding, straight-forward and not hold anything back. I promise to tell the truth, the whole truth and nothing but the truth. I promise to tell you things that you may not want to hear. I promise to tell you things you need to hear. I promise you will be enlightened by our conversation. I promise to make this a life-changing experience. This is because I speak with such passion. So if my passion/ aggression bothers you don't bother even reading this book! No, I am just playing! Putting that aside, and giving you heads up. I want you to have this gift, and look at it as your little "pick me up" whenever you need it. So, take this, put it in your purse (if you have a hard copy, see how cute and convenient it is to carry) to take with you wherever you go. Okay girlfriend? And on that note, grab your wine, have a seat, and if you are relaxed, let's start chatting.

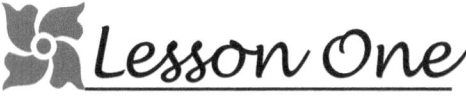

Lesson One

Defining that defining moment

Like you, I have always thought myself to be different from most. From the outside I seem like the typical person, all of my features are pleasant and pretty, I am healthy, active and productive member of society and of a family. But in truth, I'm not typical. Nothing could be further from the truth than calling me typical. I've been an oddball, unusable, unapproachable and been considered a mean girl. This is mainly because it is hard to get to know me, pin down or figure me out, and so I come off as (distant) or mean. I am constantly leaving people confused about me. My crazy personality frustrates many while it intrigues few.

I've always done things appearing far from the normal or the usual way that they are "supposed to be." Doing things "backwards" seems to be my way of operation. That is just the way that I am. As I get older I have come to realize that this much is true, I may be a bit odd and backwards. But all the while being different, I have a sense of longing for true happiness and fulfillment, like everybody else. This is something I struggled with all my life and continue to do so. It is this deep desire for happiness and a sense of fulfillment that has started me on this journey. I believe it with all of my heart, mind, body and soul that God has a designed purpose for me, and I am ready to discover this plan for my life. Like many, I have wondered about life aimlessly in search of self, and to be quite honest I still am not certain what I am looking for. What I do know is that I am beginning to understand the meaning of life, ready to embrace it, and let it transform me. At least I "think" I am ready for that transformation. In life, we will never really know why we are placed here on this earth. However, having some understanding makes being here on this earth school worthwhile, this was my revelation. I wish I would have come to this conclusion earlier on in life, but that's how life goes. You live, you learn, and in that order. This is the process of life. First experiences, lessons, then development and growth. I want to start this process by leaving you with a quote. "You can't know where you are going until you know where you've been" ~ George Santayana. This is something that I live by. So with that said, this is how the story goes.

The Defining Moment . . . .

What am I doing? What is my purpose? Why was I placed here on this earth? Asking myself these questions as I laid in bed one night thinking. All of these questions derived from the conversations of family members, friends and others whom I have had encounters with. I vividly recall the loud and echoing words "you need to find a man to take care of you, a woman place is in the house and taking care of her family, why are you going to school, you need to just to settle down and be content. "If you are going to work, find a regular job, they say. Be realistic and drop all the expectations, they say. Leave the pipe dreams alone, they say. Get your head out of the clouds, they say." They say, they say, they say. My world just became consumed with the he-sayers, she-sayers, and the rest of all the other naysayers. Although, I was clearly hearing what everyone was "saying," I still could not shake this feeling that they were all wrong. Perhaps, I was the one that was all wrong, and just did not see it. Aside from the advice, I still felt this deep longing for something more, something better, something bigger, and something grander. Am I being unrealistic and selfish? I had to ask myself. If I was being selfish, I certainly did not want to be. The self-questions then really began to fester in my mind, and why was it so difficult for me to grasp this "reality" concept?

Looking around and seeing everyone I knew, and how content they were with their mediocre lives, was absolutely puzzling to me. While this mediocrity didn't seem to bother others, it really bugged the hell out of me. It's not that I thought I was any better, but that I did not want to be like them, mediocre, bored. I really began to think that something was wrong with me. What is wrong with me, I asked myself? There has to be a better way, I thought. Am I the only one who feels this way, I often wondered? Maybe I needed to get a grip on this notion of reality before my life slipped away.

The Aha Moment . . . .

While engaged in this draining thought process, something hit me hard like a ton of bricks. Smack dab right upside the head and to the skull with the bricks. Knocking me out. When I regained consciousness, I was immediately awakened from the boisterous sounds of the critics. In spite of what everyone told me about whom I should be, and should not be, I noticed they left out one important thing. They failed to tell me that I should be happy. The

Aha moment was me realizing that those negative thoughts were not mine, but vicarious messages that unknowingly seeped into my brain and resonated deep within my psyche, and this gave me great solace. How did I completely allow the ideas and opinions of others to control my thoughts? They had managed to do a number on me. And a job well done, I'll add. It was while I was at this defining moment that lightning struck me, figuratively speaking. It struck some sense into me. Here I was thinking that I was the crazy one, and that something was wrong with me. When all alone I was perfectly sane. Their crazy ones, I thought. Ain't nothing wrong me wanting a different life! I didn't see a problem with that. The problem was not me, but with people who were trying to discourage me from pursuing a different life. Why would I allow them to do that? But that was okay because I woke up to see the light. I decided to no longer let people's opinions dictate my life. I made a conscious choice that I was going to find success. In doing just that, no one, and I mean no one was going to stop me. So, the quest began.

I am not what people say that I am. Saying these words to myself as I sat in bed staring at the ceiling. This was something that I battled with, through all the growing pains, the confusion, the disappointments, the failure, and the many unpleasant experiences. I completely ignored this while moving along in this thing called life. I became accustomed to the idea of myself influenced by people and society. However, the realistic part of me needed to understand that it was those common views that formed my life experiences. When I really think about it, all of the thoughts I had about myself can be attributed to societal views. There, I stood another victim of falling into the trap. I'm talking about that position self to fit into society trap. No longer did I want to remain in this trap. I desperately wanted out of the trap. Release me, release me, anxiously screaming I refuse to let you take me. You will not get me to serve the death sentence in that prison of misery. I was not going down without a fight. The more society tried to knock me down, the more I kept fighting. So I fought, fought, fought. Combating with the strong forceful elements of society became exhausting. It seems like the more I fought, the stronger the forces got. So, I surrendered. Dropped the weapon, hands thrown up, surrendered. It finally beat me, fair and square, society won control over me. Ultimately, I ended up in that prison of misery. Shackled and caged up behind those bars, locked away from my destiny

I could hear those voices again. The voices of those critics and the naysayers, saying "your dreams are over, join me." It felt bad being locked behind those bars. Day in and day out, the same routine. Get up, shower, get dressed and go out into the world of confinement and social conformity. Expected to go out there with all smiles and put on a happy face. Faking, fronting, and pretending, I became a pro. It was almost criminal like in that ability. But in actuality, I was sad, really, really, sad. Silently praying, wishing and hoping for something different. Something new. Something exciting. Something just for me. Are you serious? How dare you be different? These were the thoughts in my head. You aren't any different, you're just like everyone else, and the voices spoke back. Your being is expected to reflect from others and blend into the background. You want me to blend, I asked? Yes, blend it replied. Like orange jumpsuit blend? Like a shadow on the prison wall blend? Why must I blend? I did not want to live in the shadows of no man other than God. I tried blending into the background but was too bright. Hey, pointing directly to you, inmate number 436, and society is calling out to you. It was that prison life. I wasn't about that life, had to get out of there, which was not for me. I finally mustered the courage to do just that, to break free. I escaped from that prison of misery, broke the chain, stole the key, unlock that door and RAN straight for my sanity. I left people behind. I didn't look back. I didn't care anymore to see. I took off. Ran so fast. I was running to my destiny.

The Freeing moment . . .

My advice to you is RUN girlfriend. Run like the wind and save yourself before it comes searching for you. Don't let them get you as they caught me. Free yourself now. What are we running from? We are escaping society. Escaping the fact that us women have been placed in a specific category define by society and our "place" in this world, so to speak. Escaping the mundane, normal, usual, boredom, routine and mediocrity. Escaping the critics, haters, him Sayers, her Sayers, naysayers, and doubters. Escaping the predictable and inevitable. Escaping the misery. Escaping the sadness and unhappiness. Escaping societal expectations. Escaping mental enslavement and entrapment. Escaping our "female" roles.

We are running away from it all. Besides, who in the hell are they (SOCIETY) to tell us what to be? Right? How dare they? What gives them the right, I say! Well, they feel that because you are a woman, you really don't have much say so. You are expected to shut up and play your positional role. Sit down and obey to the demands of the natural law. You are to do as society commands. Besides, you are part of a society. Don't you dare stand out! Don't you dare be different! Don't you dare to dare! Didn't society tell you to BLEND? Well, Blend! Why not? They will talk about you if you don't. You don't want them to talk about you, do you? Wrong! I will stop those thoughts right there. We should not care about what they say. Girl, who gives a flying Frisbee what people say about us? Let them talk. They are going to do it anyway. We might as well give them something to talk about. We no longer care about other people's thoughts. We are dismissing those thoughts. Ladies, we are BEYOND THOSE THOUGHTS. No longer will we allow them to destroy us. No longer will we allow them to holds us back. No longer will we submit willingly to that societal placement in life which is telling us to be a "Woman."

The "Female" Moment . . . .

A woman is to be the creator and giver of life, next to God! She expects to take care of the man and be the homemaker. She expects to nurse the family when sick, as the duty of a doctor. She expects to fix problems and create solutions, as the duty of a counselor. She expects to put clothes on her family's backs, as duties of the seamstress. She expects to prepare meals and feed their bellies, as duty of the cook. She expects to provide a clean and safe living environment and maintain up keeping of the household, as the duty of a maid. She expects to provide sources of comfort, pleasure, enjoyment and contribute to happiness as the duty of an entertainer. She wears many, many, hats. Her duties aren't compensated. Her duties are tiresome. Her duties are never ending. Sometimes her duties go unrecognized. Sometimes her duties are disregarded. Sometimes her duties are unappreciated. Her work schedule is not a typical 9-5. There is no clock in, clock out, swipe the timecard schedule. Her job does not come with a hefty and attractive benefits package. There are no pay incentives, overtime pay, sick days, sick leave, or vacation. Her job is 365 days of the year, 24 hours a day, non-stop. She is a hard worker on the job. She is a team player. She is dedicated to the tasks at hand. So, with that being said, shut up! You should conform and perform your duties as society says.

WOW! Wait! Stop! Pause! And take a step back and a deep breath! Did I just described your life? Yeah, this is definitely my life in a nutshell, Ms. Davis! I had no idea you felt this way. You always keep things so bottled up. Well, don't get me wrong. Oh, how I love my job of being a mother and love my kids wholeheartedly, there are days when I feel that maybe I should have waited. Was I really ready for motherhood? Did I fully prepare for this? I guess I could answer my own questions, maybe not! But the good thing I can say about being a mother is that there is an unexplainable feeling knowing that there are little people (Children) who need you and depend on you for survival. The fact that regardless of whom you are and what you do, you aren't judge, and your mistakes and shortcomings are always forgiven. People who understand that you don't have to be perfect but still love you for you. With children, you don't have to try to impress or be something you are not. They have no concerns about that. Children are unbiased and loving human beings. They give unconditional love. I will admit it feels good when my children look at me and say "mommy" we love you. Makes me feel special. Makes me feel as if I have done something right in this life. Even in those times when I feel that I am not my best self and don't deserve it, they still show me love. Yes, that is a really good feeling. I am smiling when I talk about them, I love them little people to the death of me! Blessed to have them in my life. Keenen and Kelden, mommy loves you.

The Identifying Moment . . . .

Awww that so sweet how much you love your children, yeah I hear you! So what's the problem you ask? Although, I love my babies deeply, I can't help but feel there is still a void, and a sense that I have not completely fulfilled my destiny. What is missing? Something is missing in my life. I am sitting here with missing pieces trying to put this puzzle together. I need to find those missing pieces to complete this puzzle. That's why I have you here girlfriend, to converse with. Together we will figure this thing out, I am sure. Enough about me. Now diverting the attention away from me, let me ask you something girlfriend. Who is taking care of you? When do you have time for yourself? Ladies, you have so many things going on. Who is caring for you when you are busy taking care of everything and everyone? Don't you have a life too? Or are you vicariously living through your children? Is this really your destiny? Is this what your life is all about? Is this what you were called to do? How exciting can this be? Are you happy?

Ladies reading this, please don't take offense to what I am saying. I am in no way implying that these duties are not ours to uphold. Yes, indeed we are to be mothers, wives, child bearers, and nurturers by nature. It would be unrealistic in saying that this is not god's design for us as the female species. However, that is not gods ONLY purpose for us. I am expressing that we are not to forget about ourselves in the process. Did we forget about ourselves, all the while performing our duties and being everything to everyone else? "Momma gotta have a life too!" Quoting the movie "Baby Boy." Ladies, when is it your turn to do things just for you? We need not ignore our own wants, needs, hopes, dreams, and desires. Let me say that if being a wife, mother, and homemaker is your ultimate goal, destiny and brings you true happiness, then I am truly happy for you because ultimately this book is about finding your purpose. I am not here to judge or criticize anyone. No ma'am, not at all. I am simply here to help those who wholeheartedly believe that there is a more meaningful and purpose filled life awaiting their arrival. Do you get it?

The bad thing is that somewhere along the lines of role assignments and societal placements, people got it all twisted. Due to this, ladies we are stuck in mind frames that keep us shackled. We are fighting hard to escape. In cave man times, we were given roles to play in society. It was unacceptable for a woman to perform duties outside of the household. When a woman chose to perform duties outside the household, she was frowned upon and ridiculed. She was immediately discouraged from doing so. It is unfortunate that assigned roles has influenced the negative perception that we women sometimes have about ourselves. We have been taught to believe that we are weak, unintelligent, not smart, incompetent, incapable and inferior. It is this negative image that holds us back in life and keep from true happiness. Without a doubt I believe once we change our mentality, we will change this world.

It is a sad thing to witness our generation of women be completely brainwashed by the ridiculous concepts society has imposed upon us. At the same time, this is at no fault of our own but simply the fact that this is what was depicted by our elders and our history. However, this is not to place blame on them for they were taught by their elders, and so on, and so forth. Until we wise up, and take responsibility for our own lives and happiness, the cycle of misery will most likely continue to repeat itself. There are so many women in today's society crippled by the stigmas of worthlessness every day. Women are suffering from the feeling that we have no special place in this world. This needs to ends today, and right now at this identifying moment. Plain and simple, society has screwed our world up.

As a result, we women disgrace, dishonor, and depreciate ourselves in the most unspeakable ways. We are not living up to our best potential. We devalue ourselves in thoughts that we think, the words that we speak, and our actions by the things that we do. We blatantly ignore and fail to follow our intuition, good common sense, heart and knowledge. This ultimately leads us in the wrong directions. We ladies were not put on earth to be merely servants. I don't think so. We are special. We all have unique purposes. It is time that we live with such purposes. Live the life that God has designed for you, my friend are you ready?

In the moment . . . .

I've had enough of the put downs, disregards, and stereotypes. Ladies, now is the time we do away with the negativity, criticism, disapproval and condemnation. It is our time to shine like the stars that we are. Enough of feeling like we aren't good enough. No more thoughts of being inferior and feeling less than. Our moment is here to take this entire world by storm. No more ignoring our own hopes, desires and dreams. No more putting others needs ahead of our own. No more self-doubt. No more self-pity. No more feeling sorry for self. No more of sadness, and unhappiness. No more mediocrity.

No more watching our dreams float on by. No more watching others dream come true. Time for a change!

Why not let that time be right now? Change! You deserve the life of your dreams. You deserve happiness. You deserve passion. You deserve fulfillment. You deserve greatness. Happiness is your birthright! Passion is the birthplace! Fulfillment is the calling! And the Greatness is your destiny! Ladies, what is your defining moment? Let this be your defining moment. If you want to take this journey of self-discovery, passion, enjoyment, thrill, fulfillment, success and happiness, put your shoes on, tie them up, and we will walk into our destiny together, are you ready?

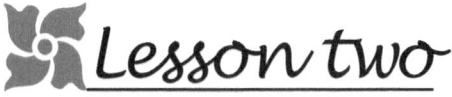

Lesson two

Finding you in the process

Girl what are you talking about find me in the process? I know whom I am, and what makes you think that I don't know myself? Well, let me put it this way. Reading this guide, aren't you? Enough said! That tells me you need some help with attempting to evaluate who you are, and what will make you happy. In that assessment, wouldn't I be correct? I hear lip smacking and see eyes rolling. I warned you in the beginning that I wasn't going to hold anything back, remember that? Ha-ha, I'm just kidding ladies. I had to start this new lesson off on a lighter note because it's bout to get serious.

Why do we need to find ourselves in the process? The answer is quite simple. If one has no idea of whom they are, how can one possibly know what one wants? Wouldn't you agree? Of course I will admit that this is easier said than done, knowing oneself that is. To be completely frank with you, there are no guarantees that you will find this out by the end of this book. But the information, and advice I am providing will help you in a step toward that direction. The finding you in the process is just that, a process! Step one in finding you in the process is self-reflection. It is imperative in search for self that you dedicate yourself to do some soul searching.

17

Soul searching consists of strategic probing, deep digging, diligent contemplating, effective assessing, assertive evaluating, and necessary isolating. It requires going to the core, and root of your being. This is the best way to describe it. Like a tree trying to grow. The big pretty tree that you see with the colorful and healthy leaves. The tree starts from the root, and grows from the ground up.

For a moment, picture yourself as a tree. Before you even begin to plant a tree. You need a location, a designated spot, the ground, dirt of course, the right temperature, plant, and a shovel to dig the hole. Grab the shovel, let's get to digging! Come on DIG, deep, deep girl! Whew sound like of work eh? (Wipes forehead). Just a bit! No one said this was going to be easy, but it is definitely well worth it. Therefore, if you do the work the rewards will be great and you will be able to sit back, and reap the benefits of your hard work. Roll up your sleeves my friend, we are about to go to work. Hope you aren't afraid of a little labor.

Self-Search . . .

Knowing whom I am and finding myself was not an easy road for me, no, no, not at all. Candidly speaking, I don't even remember seeing the damn road. As easy as I wanted things to be, they simply were not. Unlike myself, some people cheat themselves out of an experience, and take the quick and easy way out. Not me, I traveled through the mud, rocks, gravel, dirt and dust to get to where I am today. I am grateful that I did. There were no short cuts, alleyways, side streets, or express lanes to get me there faster. By my own will, I decided to take the long route, very slowly, traffic jammed, red lights, stop lights, do not enter, stop here, proceed with caution, right turn only, one lane, car blowing, angry road rage drivers yelling lady get your ass out of the way route to the destination. I know what you are thinking. I should have asked someone for directions, maybe? Better yet, I should have gotten me a GPS navigation system or MapQuest, right?

Yeah, well I agree, but do you remember me telling you that thing about doing things my own way? That most certainly was the case (shaking my head). I decided to take a chance on getting lost. I threw away the directions and just went. Car windows foggy from the rain (tears), wheels wobbling (hesitation), and what's that noise, is that the engine knocking (confusion)? Whelp, oh well, I will check it later. While it would have been smart to stop and check to see what the noise was, I kept on rolling. Ignoring the fact that I could possibly break down on the side of the road, and need to call for assistance, was a risk I was willing to take.

While in motion, I had absolutely no idea where I was going, and not an actual destination. I just went! I was unconcerned for my safety while riding along an unfamiliar path. It did matter to me, all I knew was that I needed to take that ride. I had to clear my mind. I had to clear those THOUGHTS. I had to get away from people, and I needed to get myself together. Believe it or not there are some days I still take that long drive. The good news is, through all of that exhausting commuting, I have come very close to self-discovery. Coming close, is absolutely a tremendous breakthrough for me. However, I understand that commuting through rocks, gravel, dirt and dust may not be your idea of traveling, I get that. But what you need to understand is that sometimes it is perfectly alright to get dirty. Sometimes you have to get down in the dirt, and sift through all of the unpleasant things to find what you are looking for. Get to point? The point is if you do not look hard for your destiny, you may never find it. While you are looking for your purpose be sure to chart your own course. Take your own path. Go your own way. Try a new route. Let the wind blow whichever way it may. Just roll with it. I am not telling you to not have a plan or seek directions, but sometimes you just have to explore. We can't always plan everything in life. Sometimes we have to learn to just follow our intuition, and let it guide us where ever it may. Hopefully, it leads us in the right direction. If you have that feeling to just go, do not fight it. Put yourself out there. Have faith that you will get there safe and sound. Put the pedal to the medal and Go.

How to find you . . .

Follow up question! Ms. Davis how are you suggesting I go about this "self-discovery"? Well friend, please don't get mad at me, but I don't have fool proof answers for that. Well, what the hell am I good for? While I can't tell you that this will definitely work, I can tell you what I did that worked for me. I can only hope it does the same for you. Some of the things that I will mention you may find somewhat odd and unusual. I'll admit that some of those thing were strange. First, and foremost I needed time to myself. When anyone is going through any kind of process, the first thing they need to do is have alone time to think. When I was going through the find me in the process, I had to focus on me. Therefore, I completely caged, sheltered, distance and isolated myself from the outside world. I distance myself from everyone and everything. I just needed time to think. Think, think, think and more thinking! My mind became dominated with thoughts of change. Change, change,

change! Sometimes, I just grew tired of the constant thoughts. I was obsessed and desperate with trying to figure my way out. For the most part, this didn't do anything but give me plenty of headaches. I can recall spending countless hours secluded in my room with the lights out, sitting in the dark, and hoping that the bright light bulb idea would go off right above my head. What? Did I say something funny? Oh my! Silly me! I know this sounds so absurd, but hey it seems to work in the movies.

Get to the point already? Ok! Calm down I am getting there. My point is there are some uncomfortable and even strange things that you may have to do to find you in the process. Naturally, people will think that you have lost your ever-loving mind. How could you blame them? I would think you have gone coo-coo too when sitting alone in dark rooms, staring at ceilings, waiting for imaginary glowing lights and stuff. Am I suggesting that you do this? No, I am not suggesting you do this. Not really! Well, okay, maybe I am. If that's what it takes. I am telling you to pay those people no never mind for they are obviously unaware of the finding you process. Forget people, do what you have to do! This is the time you are focusing just on yourself. Please understand that this part in the finding you process is necessary for the changes you are seeking. It will do you some good, trust me, you will thank me later. In that searching process, I can honestly say I have tried all sorts of things imaginable, some good and not so good. Eventually, they worked together to help me find what I was searching for. However, there are some helpful things that I would like to suggest that may help you in your journey, which include reading astrology, positive mantras and self-help books such as this one. Praying, meditating, reflecting, and writing are also creative outlets. I am still currently attempting to master the art of meditating, so I can't give you definite instructions on that, you will have to learn this on your own. However, you may find some of these things to be effective in nature, it all just depends on what you are comfortable with. Many of them do work. There is no harm in at least giving them a try, what do you have to lose?

Destiny in the stars . . .

Did she just say to read Astrology? What if I did? Is something wrong with that? No, I am not crazy. Please hear me out. Believe it or not reading astrology has helped me. I learned so much about myself, characteristics, personality traits, likes and dislikes, from reading astrology. I learned the reasons why I do the things that I do. I learned the reason why I think the way that I think and why I am the way that I am. It helped me to clarify and clearly define what I had been internalizing but could not quite explain, put my finger on nor pin point. Reading astrology on a daily basis gave me eye opening insight on a lot of things. I felt a deep connection to what it explained, and it all made sense. It was like having an AHA epiphany moment, every time I read it. The more I read, the more things began to make sense. I could understand myself better. I wasn't as confused as I had been before. And you are telling me you got that from reading astrology? Ummmm. Yes, I am! I know what you are thinking. You don't even have to say it. The first thing people think when I explain to them my love for astrology is that I am crazy. I suppose you think that too? I am quite sure you are really thinking to yourself that this girl's officially some type of a nut. But not just any nut, I am an acorn off the tree type of a nut, don't you think? LOL. No, I don't think I am not a nut. I will tell you that there is a lot of truth to that astrology stuff.

For example, the Pisces zodiac sign, my zodiac sign, I learned that I am thoughtful, creative, imaginative, free-spirited, exciting, adventurous, lively, entertaining, fun, spontaneous, zestful, risk taking, and full of life. On the flip side, I am sensitive, emotional, unconventional, intuitive, spiritual, flightiness and sometimes moody. My astrological sign also defines me as a person who needs to be engaged in careers that allow creative expressions, writing, for example. For now, we will just leave it right there. I will get into more details about my interest and activities in the *Finally out of the box* lesson after *A passion for passion.*

Bringing myself back to the point I was trying to express, it is perfectly okay to be odd and unusual. Our focus here is finding you in the process. Yep, it is official, Tameisha is a quack! Never said I wasn't girlfriend! I may be kooky, but I am HAPPY in that disposition. This brings me to my next point, don't be afraid to be you! As humans and creatures of social formality, we all have an inherent desire to be liked so much that in the process of trying to fit in and find our way, we don't fully express who we are inside. When we aren't allowed to express ourselves, it creates so much confusion within. This confusion is what causes us to be trapped in an identity crisis. When we are immensely dedicated to being what and whom we think people want us to be, we can sometimes lose sight of selves. We engage in unconscious and subconscious acts that keep us in a society filled with restraints, restrictions, confinement and standards that hold us from our ultimate purpose and fulfillment, this can be hard for one to bear at times. Say what now girl? You completely lost me on that one. I know I may have but don't trip girlfriend. I understand a sister getting real deep on ya huh? You weren't ready for that. Totally unexpected, that I know. Let me get back on track. What I am expressing is that when you are finding you in the process don't be led by others definition of you!

God did not put you here to conform, he put you here to perform, be the star of the show, that is. Before you can perform, you have to have the manuscript, an assigned role, practice and preparation, supporting cast, director, confidence, courage, bravery and the strong will to get in front of the crowd. The crowd is waiting. Roll the curtains. Say your prayer. The spotlight is beaming on you. Are you ready? Ready or not, it is show time. Don't be scared! Have no worries because you can do this. You were born for this. This part was made just for you. So what are you waiting for? Go out there! Besides, I am here to help you. I won't let you fail. I GOT YOU! Go ahead, the stage is all yours. DO YOU!

Quick Rewind . . . .

Interesting perspectives, Ms. Davis! Well, I know! My whole take on this find you in the process thing is only mentally strong individuals can recognize and admit when there is a need to discover self. Recognize it not only for the purposes of professing but because there is a real need to improve the life that God has blessed you with. More importantly, when finding you in the process, is finding you in God. I like to call it the "DIVINE." Aside from the definition, there is a magnificent and powerful force that has created the amazing being that is you. You are one of a kind. There is no other person like you in the world. You may be completely unaware of your purpose, special gifts and talents. And it is okay to be unsure. I am here to tell you we all are gifted because we are fearfully and wonderfully made. It is our obligations and responsibilities to acknowledge and endorse these talents as being beautifully tailored human elements. Taking this time to find yourself is a necessary task. You have a mission to accomplish on earth but first you have to understand what that mission is.

When you have acquired self-awareness, it will equip you with the tools needed, and you will know what needs to be done. Regardless of what you must endure, how long it takes, and how it may affect others, self-discovery is essential in living the life you are destined to live. In *finding you in the process*, we will search and find our inner strengths using the power of positive thoughts. We will delve into the depths of our creative souls. We will unravel the mystics of our wondering minds. And we will explore the spirits of our opened hearts. Is that okay? DAMN! Sounds deep! Real deep girl! I hear you! I'm sorry ladies, a girl's spiritual side kicked in, and it was good to go. Let me take a step back, because y'all ain't ready for this. LOL. Does any of this make sense? If not, do not worry! I got a whole lot more. Hold on! (Sips wine).

Ok, I'm back! I have returned from that much needed wine break. Where was I? Oh! I was saying that finding you in the process of finding your purpose is not all that bad. It actually was an experience of understanding and enlightenment, for me. It allowed me to get outside of myself, so to speak. I was able to release all of those fears and inhibitions. I was able to relax, focus, breathe and be open to explore. Sounds like floating through the clouds, you say? I'll say that it could be attributed to that experience. Personally, there is an empowering feeling when you are able to just be free. Therefore, the finding you process can be exhilarating, invigorating, uplifting inspirational. Nonetheless, each person in this process will encounter different feelings and outcomes, expecting to make oneself a better person, as a result. Please do not skip the finding you in the process step. It is much needed. We need this, as it will help us get to the next level in our journey.

Please repeat that . . . .

Huh, what did you say? Can you please repeat that? I was saying that another thing which helped me in this *find me process* was immersing myself in daily affirmations and positive mantras. Truth be told, there is an abundance of power just in the words that we speak. I will spend a lot of time on this throughout this book as this is the whole purpose of our discussion. I like to consider myself a positive mantra junkie. I simply can't get enough of them. It's like if I go one day without my mantras, I can't function. It is the constant words that keep me focused everyday and steer clear of all negative thoughts. When you speak positive words to yourself you are removing all negative and toxic thoughts from the mind, and allowing the flow of positivity and creativity. It helps to both say and read words of affirmation aloud. It is said that we respond better to both visual and audio messages. Therefore, hearing the words (audio) and seeing them (visual) is most effective. Here's a little exercise, try this one on for size. I want you to repeat after me. "I am smart. I am intelligent. I am creative. I am beautiful. I am loving. I am unique. I am special. I am amazing." I couldn't hear you, please repeat that. "I am smart. I am intelligent. I am creative. I am beautiful. I am loving. I am unique. I am special. I am amazing."

Now did you hear that? How does that sound? It sounds good, right. How does it feel? Don't you feel those words? Don't you feel powerful and unstoppable? Exactly! The more you do this, the more you will actually start to feel this way. Be sure to make this a habit. The first step to changing your thoughts, is changing your words.

Repeated affirmations help to bring positive energy in and drawing negative energy OUT. Positive words are that protective shield that automatically blocks out the negative energy. We want that positive energy disseminated throughout our bodies. This in turn, make us feel better. We feel better when we think better. We do better when we act better. And so on and so forth. But for now let's stop there as we continue on to connecting with the divine. We will resume our conversation on positive thoughts and affirmations in the *it's a mind thing* lesson toward the end of our discussion.

Connect with the Divine . . .

Prayer is also useful in the self-discovery and finding you in the process. This consists of simply clearing your mind, and connecting with the divine intelligence for wisdom, and guidance. You can call this God, force of nature, or whatever you like, but it involves relinquishing, and surrendering all of your "control" to that which has the ULTIMATE control. This too requires a bit of solitude and space for allowing that creative force to manifest itself. Normally, people picture prayer as a kneeling on all fours, head bowed, hands folded, biblical language speaking kind of ritual. This isn't necessarily what it entails. It is actually an intimate conversation and stillness with the higher power. It is a one on one informal talk which helps you to connect with the divine. In this prayer process we are developing a personal relationship with "God." What we are hoping to receive from this connection is that we provided with guidance, courage, wisdom, knowledge or whatever we desire. I can tell you that it is very helpful, therapeutic, and can also be a good release. Alright! Alright! Alright! A sister's spiritual side intruding again, and it has completely taken over.

Now do you see where I am coming from? I hope so. Yes, I had to break it all the way down, you feel me? But as I said before, it all really depends on what you are most comfortable with. Different strokes for different folks. I am not imposing my ideas on youthese are merely suggestions. All this find you in the process is nice but what do you do after you have done so? That is the million dollar question! After you have developed some idea of who you are, the next step is to focus on your passions. What are they? Do you have any? Of course, we all do! Ladies let us make our passions come alive in this next lesson. "A passion for passion."

Lesson three

A passion for passion

What is passion? Exactly what does this mean, you ask? What do you mean by you have a passion for passion? That's just crazy. I feel you! I'll explain it to you, give me one second. But before we begin, let me stop for a refill (pours wine). Ok, my glass is ready and filled, how about yours? We were talking about passion, is that right? Well, to me, passion is that thing that tugs at your heart, soul, and mind all at the same time. It is a feeling of fulfillment. It is an unexplainable feeling of joy.

For example, when we are hungry, and our stomach is growling, we eat food to fill our belly and satisfy the hunger. Passion is something like that. It is that full feeling deep with our being. Passion is what makes you come alive. Without passion you are living but are not ALIVE. Passion can come from anything. Just think for a moment. What is that thing that makes you feel alive? It can be love. It can be an activity. It can be a place, person, or thing. Did you instantly become happy when you thought about that thing? If you did not get excited, then that was not your passion, my dear. Your passion will actually ignite a fire in you like fuel to a flame. So, Ms. Davis what are the things that set you on FIRE!!!?

Love me passionately . . .

"Some people are in love with love." This is a statement that totally describes me. I am extremely passionate about love. The idea of it alone just makes me smile. Call me that hopeless romantic. Yet, I have failed to find that "love" that I've been searching for. You will most likely find me to be that one crying along to those television, Cinderella, snow white, fairy-tail, and happily ever after type of love stories. Since I was a little girl, I have always dreamed of being whisked away on a horse and carriage by my knight and shining armor. We would ride off into the midnight, go get hitched, and the rest will be history. Laughing out loud! Yes once again, I know, silly me! Only if you could see my face right now, just talking about it makes me light up like a Christmas tree. What does all this have to do with passion? Everything! Love sets the foundation for happiness which contributes to positive thoughts. I may have described this storybook type of love which is very far fetched.

But in reality, there is a type of love attainable for true happiness. It is called self-love. Self-love is real. Self-love is achievable. Self-love is necessary. It is important we learn how this self-love thing works, for the changes needed to improve our lives. What does this have to do with passion, once again? Ladies you need to develop a PASSION FOR SELF. You need to love yourself so hard until it hurts. You need to love yourself beyond measures, beyond words, and beyond all conceivable thoughts. When we love ourselves, we open up our world to endless possibilities. It is that self-love that makes you realize your worth. When you realize your worth, you won't settle for anything less than you deserve. You'll seek the best in relationships, career and success. Self-loving people want nothing but the best for themselves. I will tell you that when you don't love yourself, it can be hard to love anyone or anything. This special love comes from within.

Some will likely attribute this "self-love" to a feeling from outwardly appearance. It will have some influence, but this is not what it entails. Self-love doesn't mean that you have to look or be perfect. Absolutely not, it's about loving yourself despite your flaws, imperfections, and shortcomings. It is seeing nothing but the best in yourself, and looking beyond all imperfections. Self-love isn't negative, critical, or judgmental. It requires an authentic and genuine care for oneself. We ladies need to do more of this self-love thing, and give it to ourselves unconditionally. Do you feel me ladies? If you don't already, learn to do this. This is something that I definitely had to learn for myself.

I was once at a point in my life when I really did not love or like myself. Unsatisfied with my looks, criticizing my body, and doubting my abilities, were all negative behaviors within my existence. I had a hard time with actually loving myself authentically. I spent so much time trying to change everything I didn't like about myself. I wasn't trying to change for the better, as I should have. Yet, I tried to change into something I was not. I thought that things would be different in my life, if I changed who I was. Besides, I needed a change. I was tired of the *same ol me*.

I was a fool! This did not work. It made matters worse. There I was, so lost, and had no clue who the hell I was. I do not want to put the blame on anyone, but society, media, and the likes contributed towards this critical negative self-image, self-doubt, and self-hatred.

Society made me do it. Yeah, it was society's fault. It made me change who I was. I had become preoccupied with looking at other women, and disliking myself. I felt as though I was not like what appeared to be in eyes as "perfect." I failed to realize that there was no such thing as perfection. Those women I compared myself to were no better than me, and just as flawed. I ignored the fact that they were also human. Eventually, this constant comparison caused great despair and sadness. This was an awful state to be in, and it did nothing to help me in the process.

Truthfully, I believe that there has been a point in every woman's life when she has played the competition game. One reason we compete is because we are jealous, hateful and envious of one another, especially black women. Yes, I said it! Most black women are jealous of one another. Black women have this notion, "I got to be better than you" and "if I am winning, you are losing." This is a ridiculous notion that we have invented in our own heads. It just doesn't make any sense. What a waste of both time and thoughts! In actuality, we are too busy trying to be one step ahead in a race that we all are losing. What I mean by that is, when one of us ladies is down this affects all of us. Let's stop the competitions. Let's all run in the same race. Ladies we all can win. We all can be successful. We all can accomplish our goals. Together, we can be victorious. But first we need to stop wishing and comparing ourselves to one another. When we stop the comparisons, we can actually focus on ourselves. It is this comparison that keeps us from recognizing our own uniqueness and individuality. How can you focus on yourself when you are too concerned with someone else? I'll answer that. You can't. This competition does nothing to help you in progress and forward movement. Comparison, envy, and jealousy are like debilitating illnesses that will keep you immobile, stuck, and unproductive. If ignored, undiagnosed, and left untreated, it can spread to other areas of your life. Eventually, this will affect your success and happiness. Ultimately, this is not good for you. I am sure this is not what you want.

Another thing we must do is stop is letting society manipulate us into thinking we have to be against each other. We are not enemies, we are one of the same. There is unnecessary separation and division between us. We should come together. We should be for each other. Ladies, this is one reason I wanted to write this book. I am doing this in the spirit of sisterhood. I want us to unite. I want us to stop competing and start supporting. All for one and one for all, this is the togetherness that we women should strive for. We can do it.

I have come to give you some good news. Sure, I'll share! There is a cure for this jealousy illness. Is there really a cure "Doc"? And if so can you write me up a prescription? Yes, of course, fortunately there is, and that cure is called self-love. I am advising you to administer it to yourself every day, all-day, for the rest of your life. You will start to feel better at the very first dose. I promise you! Try it or yourself. If you don't start to feel result instantaneously, just keep taking it, and eventually it will kick in. Don't worry about an overdose! There is no harmful side effects. Actually, it's an all-natural sustenance. However, results may vary. Now we're talking about taking medication, Ms. Davis? What's next? I know girl, I'm a mess! So wrapping up this lesson, let us backtrack for a moment. Self-love comes from "defining yourself" and "finding yourself" as we mentioned in previous lessons.

To recap what we've been discussing. In the *defining moment* lesson we discussed whom you are as it relates to society. In the *finding you in the process* lesson, we discussed God's purpose for the amazing being that is you. Now in this *passion for passion* lesson we are focusing on self-love, success and happiness. Gosh, that was a lot of information. I agree, but I have no doubt that you absorbed it all. While we did spend quite a bit of time talking about self-love, it is time to get into the topic of finding your passions in success and happiness. Do you need a break? Go ahead, but come back. Don't worry, I'll wait.

Find your passions . . .

What are you good at? What do you love to do? What strike your interests? Do you need time to think about this? I understand, this make take some time to think about or maybe not. No pressure! Take your time. Let me see if I can help you here identify what some of those passions might be. First off, let me tell you that everyone is good at something. Before those thoughts even enter your mind, it does not have to be some BIG thing. It is the simplest thing you could be talented at. I will start with myself. I am good at making others feel good. I am a good listener, and can relate to the needs of others. I have a natural gift for helping and nurturing people. This is something I love to do. I am compassionate, thoughtful and giving. I love learning, reading, studying, and writing, my favorite things to do. These are just a few examples to give you some idea. Does that get you to thinking about your talents and gifts, now? I hope it does.

Going back to this passion thing, as you were thinking of your skills and interest,did any of them strike or touch a soft spot in your body? If you felt a spark, you may have found your passion. When you are passionate about something, there is enjoyment in doing it. It will be exciting for you to be engaged in it. After all, who wouldn't prefer to do something that is enjoyable? Passion is what keeps you excited, thrilled and interested in a particular thing. You will know when you are passionate about something.

When you are passionate about something, the pain of not doing it, will be as painful as doing it. When you are passionate about something, no one or nothing can keep you from it. Like a bee to a flower, you will become drawn to it. Like a pin to a magnet, you will be attached to it. It will be hard not to attract in some way. It will find a way to show up in your life at any time and all the time. Of course, you may never notice it or pay attention to it, but it is always there. From the time we are born, passions choose us, we do not choose them. Our job is taking the time to acknowledge and develop them. Do you remember when we talked about that tree in *finding you in the process?* Yes, exactly like that. Our passions are like trees. If we want our passions to grow, and develop into useful things, we must plant the seeds, water them, and nurture them. Do you agree?

It was as though I fell in love for the first time when I found my passion. Head over heels! Like love at first sight. Like butterfly feeling in the stomach, in love. When I was not engaged in my passion, things were really difficult for me. I had to be with passion all the time. But passion and I had a funny relationship. It didn't want me, when I wanted it. And I didn't want it, when it wanted me. However, when we were apart, I could hardly function, focus, and concentrate. I was a walking zombie without it. It was like having no air supply and unable to breathe. I needed that oxygen. We all need oxygen. One day, we decided to be together seriously, and we have been happy ever since.

Look at your passions like those things you can't live without. Become one with your passions. Develop a love for your passions. Let passions be your everything. Let passions be all that you need. Let passions into your life. Don't push them away! Invite them to stay. Open your heart to your passions. Open your mind to your passions. Open your soul to your passions. Besides, y'all were meant to be together, you and passions fit. Call me the love doctor. I am matching you up with passions. No need to thank me! I am doing this for you. Do you like passions? Aren't passions wonderful? Don't they take your breath away? Let your passions take your breath away. Inhale, now exhale, and breathe! That's call PASSION, feels good, doesn't it?

Passion for Success . . . .

What do you mean by your passion for success? Well, what I mean by that is, for as long as I can remember, I knew that I would be successful one day. It was this intuition that always told me this. You can call it my passion for success. However, my actions and mind could never seem to get on the same accord. I had this intuition, and for years it tried hard to get my attention. It poked at me. It whistled at me. It tried to flag me down. But being the stubborn person I am, I didn't want to listen, or pay attention, so it was ignored.

What intuition am I referring to? I am referring to the messages that guide you to your destined path, and life's purpose. I am talking about the message that are sent from God. We are given the signs early on. Sometimes we choose to ignore them, and I did. Big mistakes! God gave me the dream a long time ago. But the visions are just now becoming clear. It took me a long time to understand that, but I finally get it. I am listening DIVINE, and following your lead. Normally, this happens as you move closer to your destiny. I believe, from the time we are born, we are destined for success, as it chooses us. The good news is we all will be chosen for different reasons. I think I was specifically chosen to help and inspire people. I believe this is God's purpose for me.

In my adult life, I have taken many different directions in pursuit of success. I think at least several different paths may have been chosen. I think I needed to follow different paths to determine which one was the best for me. "Girl, you don't know what you want to do with your life." I had become use and accustomed to hearing this. Although this was true, it doesn't stop me from continuing to find me niche. I have gone from job to job. You name it, I have tried it. I worked in retail, absolutely hated that. I worked in public office settings, hated that. I even went to dental school, hated that, as well.

It's so frustrating going from one boring, mundane, and menial job to the next. I need to find the career that is right for me. I have to do away with the routine, confinement, set scheduling, authority and dealing with difficult people. What can I do long term? What will keep my interest? What will I be happy doing? These are question I asked myself on this path to success. I finally figure out what was missing from those jobs, CREATIVITY. Yeah, that's what I need. The lack of creativity, imagination, and self-expression in jobs are brutal for me. Those types of boring jobs felt like imprisonment to me. Actually, to say that they felt like imprisonment would be an understatement. Those jobs felt more like death. The kind of death where you are severely punished and slowly tortured until your air supply is cut off and you collapse. How would I know what death feels like? Well, I have never experienced death per say, but this is what it feels like from what I have been told. Yes! I am talking about that 9-5 work life. Sounds dreadful, huh? It most definitely is drudgery! Harsh, gruesome, *plain ol* cruel. I deserve, need, and desperately want more than this. I do not feel that this life is fit for everyone. One size does not fit all, and what is good for the goose, certainly isn't good for the gander. This is the best way to describe me in many job situations. Now why would anyone in their right mind want to subject their self to that? I just never felt any of those jobs were right for me.

Stop, before you even think that. I am not attempting to discourage you from holding a regular job. I don't want you to think that I am telling you to not work. I am simply expressing that the regular job scene is not for me, that's all. I just never felt fulfilled in those positions from my experience. I personally need to be engaged in careers that are inspiring, motivating, and exciting. I thrive on creativity, fantasy and imagination. I mostly crave careers that spark my creativity. I am a person filled with so many creative ideas. I have to let them out. Come out, come out, where ever you are!!!. What's my point? My point is you should do something you love to do. If a job doesn't make you happy, don't stay there, find one that does. Why would you stay in the misery? Don't get stuck in the drudgery, like me. Find the job right for you. "If you love what you do, you will never have to work a day in your life" ~ Confucius. I am doing exactly that, to make a long story short. So, here I am, yet again, making another detour in my pursuit of success. Next stop, Author's Ville. Why not give this author thing a shot, since I have a passion for it?

Passionately happy . . .

Even if we have not positioned ourselves in that fulfilling role and position in life, we should be happy anyways. Did someone say Happy? Yes, I said, happy! Don't worry, be happy! I just like singing that. Anyways, we will briefly talk about this happiness thing. What am I talking about "happy," you ask? How does this relate to passion? Ok, I will explain by giving you my personal definition. Happiness is an expression of both inward and outward appreciation for oneself, life, and situation, and wherever you are at this present moment. It is being grateful for all that you have, and seeing the beauty in everything.

What does this have to do with passion? Well, if you are happy with life things can become enjoyable. And when things are enjoyable, passion is likely to arise. Enjoyment leads to passion. Do you see how this works? You think this sound like perfection? No, it doesn't mean your life is perfect, or even your situations are perfect. It just means that despite the imperfections you choose to Have A Positive Personality Yet. How can you possess this happiness? I'll tell you that happiness is a choice. It is an individual choice. The choice is ultimately yours to control. It took me a very long time, and I am continuously learning to master this concept. We can choose sadness or happiness. Simple! What is happiness? Happiness is defined as a fleeting emotion that fluctuates and changes like a chameleon changes color. It comes and goes without announcement or warnings. Its fluctuations can be mild or intense. It is also defined differently by different people. Not everyone will view happiness the same. What makes one person happy, may not do the same for another. However, happiness is noticeable, and you will be able to recognize it once you feel it.

Unlike the chameleon whose changes are beyond control and variations come from its natural element, happiness comes directly from your efforts and control. There is no one or nothing that has the force or control to make you happy besides you. Well, technically God has that control, but you know what I mean. How will I know if I am happy? Happy is not your typical skip, skip, skip to my Lou, hopping and dancing around, smiling like a treasure cat, singing from the rooftop type of disposition. It appears more of a graceful, humbled, and loving appreciative demeanor. Or well at least is should.

Many times what we think may be happy is not. So don't let that "happy look" fool you. People think happy is a look. It is not. Happiness is an inner feeling. However, when we are happy it will exude outwardly. But that is irrelevant, because we aren't trying to prove our happiness to anyone. The bottom line is let happiness manifest itself in your life. What we need to work on is actually getting our thoughts, words and action in alignment to create this happiness. Once we understand that it is possible to be happy, we can learn how to achieve it. We should work every day toward this because in the end it will make our lives better.

How to be happy . . .

Do you really need instructions on how to be happy? This is such an easy task. It's not difficult. It is not rocket science. It requires no investigation or complex thinking. If you want to be happy, be grateful. Gratefulness! This is as easy as it gets. How does one be grateful, you ask? Well, if you can wake up each day and decide that you will be appreciative of life, then you can easily be grateful. Now that isn't hard to do, is it? Gratefulness contributes to positive thoughts. Positive thoughts contribute to happiness. Do you see where I am going with this? When you're appreciative and grateful for all of the things that you have in life, this open the doors of opportunity to receive more.

Do you understand how this happy thing works now? Yes, I will further explain. Okay, happiness is like learning to ride a bike, the more you practice the better you become at it. Remember your first bicycle? The one that had the training wheels to get you into practice, and preparation for the real deal. Happiness is something like that. When you take off the training wheels of doubt, uncertainty, apprehension and fear, you give yourself the opportunity to be free from that which hinders you from reaching your fullest potential. Are you ready to take off those training wheels? Go ahead, take off those training wheels. Be free, free, free, and ride off into a life of sheer bliss. WATCH OUT! As you are riding off into this happiness be sure to avoid anything that looks negative, complaining, critical and bitter. We would not want you to come into contact with any of these. Would you like to give this this happiness a try? It will become second nature once you learn to do it. Okay, I'm stepping back now, giving you some space, encouragement and letting you give it a shot. What's that, you want me to come too? Yes my friend, I will join you. I will be grabbing my bit of happiness too.

Ms. Davis, why are you so damn HAPPY? Well, I am happy because it is beneficial for overall health. I am happy because I am alive. I am happy because I am fearfully, and wonderfully made. I am happy because I am changed. I am happy because life is full of opportunities. I am happy for my future. I am happy because I am blessed. I am happy because life is a gift. And what do we do with gifts? We enjoy them. We cherish them. We value them. We appreciate them, and we are HAPPY with them. Gifts are special to us, right? Besides, it does no good to be unhappy? I would say it is pointless. Does that answer your question? I hope it does.

Well good for you Ms. Happy, you say? Call me what you want, it doesn't bother me not one bit. I am happy. Anyways, now back to you, I am not letting you off the hook. Enough procrastinating are you ready to give this happy thing a shot? No worries, you got this. You can make this happen. It is all up to you. So, get ready to be your best self. On your mark, get set, GO! Waving as you ride off.

I will be right behind you.

Lesson four

Got that covered

Well why can't I have it all? Love, family, happiness and success. Why must it be one way or the other? Why are we women even faced with this dilemma? So often, when we are dedicated to our families, we don't have outside success. If we are successful, then we must have a lack of love. If we want love, then we must sacrifice our career life. I reiterate, why can't we have it all? It seems so unfair to me that we have to choose. I don't want to give up one thing to have another. Why should I have to? What is wrong with having it all? I need someone to explain this to me. I don't understand this concept.

What's that saying ladies? You can't have your cake and eat it too. Bull crap! Watch me! Watch how I take a big bite out of it, and wash it down with vanilla some ice cream too. Besides, what is the point of having cake if you can't eat it? I always hated that saying! Here the crazy lady go again with her little brilliant analogies and metaphors. I hear you laughing. I am serious. Come on ladies, really think about, and it will make sense. I have not had the experience of running into too many women that have it all, love, family and success. When it comes down to it, this is what all of us women really want, isn't it ladies? Tell the truth! I honestly feel that no woman sits and says "I just want love. I just want family or I just want success." ALL women want, love, family and success. Wait, let me not disregard the fact that not all of us are the same. For those women who might be sensitive like myself, maybe I should rephrase that. I meant to say MOST of us women want, love, family, success. Am I politically correct now? For some strange reason, this seems so difficult to acquire, I wonder why? It is no secret that we ladies can be difficult complicated creatures of humanity. But in my opinion, our desires are so simplistic and pretty much the same. We just want love, family, and success. We want happiness! This seems pretty simple to me. Is this really too much to ask for? I don't think it is.

Ladies, do you know where we failed in actually getting what we want, and what our heart desires? Don't know? Okay, I'll tell you. We went wrong when we started putting our lives in the hand of others. Yes, that is correct. We depend on others to give us what we want. We depend on others to give us what we need. We simply are too dependent on others. Not good ladies, not good. We need to stop putting our happiness, lives, desires, wants, and needs into the hands of others. It is about time we take responsibility for our own lives and happiness. We can build the lives we want with the help, instructions and guidance from GOD. Like a carpenter building a foundation, you need to have the right materials and tools. But we are talking about building our dream lives here. In order to do that we can start by finding what we need to build. Ladies, previously we have just been using the wrong tools. You can't send a hammer to do the job of a wrench. Look down in that tool bag again, keep looking, did you find it? Yes, there it is. That's the tool we need to build what we want. You crack me up, Ms. Davis! I know girlfriend!

I am a trip! Let me not talk about tools as I am not a carpenter. My point is whatever you are trying to construct, model, make or build in your life is completely up to you. It is your responsibility to make it happen. You can do just that with the right tools. You are both the designer and architect of your life. Are you ready to build that dream life you have always wanted? Do you have the tools? Well let's get to building.

Call for Back up . . .

The most important tool we need is a support system, while we are trying to build a life of happiness, love, family and success. Can you recall me telling you not put your life in the hands of others, remember that? This is true! Please do not do this. However, we do need support. To achieve all that you want, support is needed. If you noticed, I said "support." Support consists of people helping you. Sometimes people get support confused with dependence. We should not depend on others. But we should seek help from others. There is a difference. Anyways, every human being needs help. No one can do everything on their own. It is critical that a support system is set in place. There are many times we have difficulties accomplishing what we set out to do because of the lack of support. By not having a support system, we are potentially held back.

Ladies, sometimes we are usually left out in that process while we are busy being the support system to everything else. When we have no one there for us it can be hard to bare. I am advising you to find some back up. Seek support as you attempt to have it all. I know I want it all. I am talking about love, family, happiness and success. I surely do! In order to have it all, I understand I need support. I have help, fortunately. Lots of help! People will disagree with me,and express that a selfish person, "wants it all." I beg to differ. I can have it all. I will have it all. I will not compromise on this. I will not settle. I will not be content and neither should you, ladies.

Besides, is there some written rule or law that states I can't have all that my heart desires. Show me, where is it, I want to see it. Exactly, I didn't think that there was. You think I'm living in La-La magical land of fairy-tales, and happily ever after's again, huh? I understand. It's no fairy tale, to me. I feel that if my mind can conceive it, I can achieve it. Sticky note on the forehead to self, I will stop listening to those who are telling me to be "realistic." This is my reality, and it is very different from yours. Back to this support thing. Ladies, if we surround ourselves with supportive people that encourage, we can actually achieve our goals. Unfortunately, this is a daunting tasks for some. Some people may really have to search hard for that needed support. I feel utterly blessed because I have a great and loving support system. Shining the light now on both my mom and sister. These two have been a tremendous support to me throughout my life, and I probably would not be where I am without their help.

The most important people we should seek support from is our loves ones, our family. I mentioned that my mother and sister have been motivating, caring, encouraging, loving, understanding, giving, and supporting especially in times of need. I have them to talk to and confide in. I have the emotional and financial support as well. My family has always been there for me. This is my situation but I understand not everyone is as fortunate. If you do not have this kind of support from your family try seeking it elsewhere. Support does not have to come directly from immediate family or even from "biological" ties. A spouse or mate can also be a source of support as well. A friend can give support. A neighbor can give support. A co-worker can give support. A stranger can give support. We can seek out support from anyone.

As we are discussing "support" know that there are different types of support that one will seek. They consist of emotional, mental, and financial. Relating back to creature of social formality people have needs to be met in each of these areas. When we are supported by the people we love it gives us the fuel we need to accomplish anything. This does not mean that without their love and support we can't follow our dreams. Really when it comes down to it you will still be able to do what you need to with or without their "support." However, it just makes having that support easier to accomplish things. I will add that it feels nice to have those words of inspiration, encouragements, and pats on the back along the way. I receive plenty of pats on the back. My sweet dear mother is one person who has always had my back. She is the epitome of a supportive person. She always tell me to stay focus, and that she is proud of me. She means so much to me. Yes, like any other typical mother-daughter relationship, we have had our ups and downs. We have not always seen eye to eye or agreed on everything, but she has always had my best interest at heart. She support my dreams to the fullest.

My dear sister as well. She is also my biggest supporter. Many siblings have the typical relationship of competition and drama. However, my sister and I do not have that typical sibling rivalry relationship. She is my best friend and confidant. She supports everything I do. Individuals differences of course at times, but she too has been the supporter that I need. I don't know what I would do without them. Well, Valeria and Catherine Davis, I have dedicated a section to you, get your shine on, LOL. Love you. Okay, now we identified our support system can we talk about what's been holding you back? Your goals that is.

Get out your own way . . . .

Pardon me, excuse me, beep, beep, move it along already. You are holding up the flow of things. There is one way we can succeed in life. Get out of our own way. Sometimes the thing that block our progress, success and happiness is actually ourselves. We can sometimes sabotage our own future and lives, unfortunately. I am sure no one wants to be the cause of their own misfortunes. However, there are things that we do, and we aren't even aware. I know all about getting in my own way. I have first hand, professional, and veteran experience when it comes to this. I was that person with so many fears which prevented me from doing a lot of things I wanted to do. I was scared of what people thought of me. I had a fear of failure. I feared the unknown. I feared success. I feared drawing spotlight attention. I feared rejection. I feared people. I was one fearful ass person. All of these fears caused me sabotage potentially good things for myself. Now that was a shame!

I used to play this game called the "what if" game, and I was good at it. You don't know how that games goes? Ok, it goes like this. What if I am making the wrong decision? What if this doesn't work out the way that I want it to? What if I am wasting my time? What if I fail? What if people don't like me? What if they ridicule me? All what ifs! I played the self-sabotage game pretty damn well and all by myself. First it was one "what if." That turned into another "what if." Which turned into I can't do this. Finally turned into forget this and enough, I quit. GAME OVER! Tragic! Everything I wanted to do, I didn't. Just gave up on it all. I let my mind talk me out of my destiny. Dreams, quit! Goals, quit! Progress, quit! Change, quit! Better life, quit! Better me, quit! I quit it all and easily gave up on any hope. Sat up there and sabotage everything and did not need anyone's help. Damn shame, indeed! Holding my head down in shame. I have since learned to stop, and refuse to GET IN MY OWN WAY of success. I said all that to say, you do not have to continue sabotaging all the good things that are in store for you. Don't give those negative thoughts the satisfaction. You can be beyond those negative, disrupting, and bad thoughts holding up your future. These thoughts should have no place or space in your brain. They are unwelcomed. Put them out. What are doing, don't let them sit there. Tell them that it is time that they go. Negative thoughts your visiting hours are over. No more letting those thoughts get in the way of your purpose.

Tell yourself that you can do anything. Know that you can do anything. If you have to pick a fight with your mind, do so. However, I am not a fan of violence but you better knock that negativity out. K.O. (Knock out). Understand that it will be a battle though. One in which we are determined not to lose. Do you have what it takes, to be a champ? Sure you do! You got to get in the ring (mind) with strength, bravery, and with courage, ready to fight the negative thoughts. We're not scared, right? We are focused and committed to this fight. Tell those negative thoughts to shut up or put up. Don't worry about losing you got back up, remember? So negative thoughts, bring it on, we have something for you.

Forget about it . . . .

What's that saying? "Let the past be the past?" Yes, this is true. Sometimes when we are in the process of pursuing the life we want, we are haunted by our pasts. This can also hinder us from progress and forward movement. Old experiences, people and "our ways" can keep us stuck at a standstill. Remembrances of a painful childhood, a devastating tragic event, and even old relationships, can hold us back, if we allow it. Ladies, let us forget about those things in our pasts that may prevent success. It does not matter what happened, know that you can overcome it. I believe that the most beautiful beginnings come from the most difficult pasts. No one is exempt from "life." It happens to all of us and to even the best of us. However, we can turn the triumphs to victories. Who am I to say this? I am exactly the person who can tell you this.

Friend listen up! Like, you I have had my share of experiences too. Difficult childhood upbringing, personal relationship turmoil's, trying times, and so on. Although I have not have personal tragic events in my life, I have had some things to overcome. You want stories? Sure, I'll share. First off, I grew up in a single parent home where my mom was the breadwinner, provider and nurturer, she did it all. She went to work every day to put a roof over me and my siblings head, clothes on our backs, shoes on our feet, and food on the table. She did what she could, when she could. She played the role of both mother and father. She was relentless in her duties. She was dedicated to us. She devoted her life to us and I am eternally grateful.

THANK YOU MOMMY, I ADORE YOU! My father was in and out of my life. I really never knew what it was like to have a dad. I missed out on that bonding experience with him. It was tough indeed. Was there a void in my life? Indeed? Did this affect me? Indeed! All of the things a little girl needed from a male figure, I did not received. Truth be told this caused some difficulties in my life and the decisions I have made thus far. It influenced the men that I dated, the things that I did to get attention, the rebellion, the anger, the resentment, the doubt in myself, the insecurities, the fear of being alone, need I go on? But you know what girlfriend? Nothing happened to me that has not happened to anyone else. As a grown woman I now realize that. I did not say all of that for you to feel sorry for me. Absolutely, not! I said all that to say, there is nothing you can't overcome, and as I mentioned before life happens to all of us.

The sad thing is you have grown ass people still using childhood experiences as excuses to not do something. "Oh, I did not have a dad." Oh, I grew up poor." "Oh, I was teased as child." Sob story after sob story. Pitiful, I say. What's even sadder is that they really have filled their own heads with this idea that because of those experiences they can't do any better than what they are doing. There is also this notion that "People are products of their environment, as I hear so many say." Excuse me, but that's baloney. We are not products of our environment. There may be things that influence our behaviors but that does not have to dictate what and whom we become. So, because I was fatherless and poor, I need to continue to have low self-esteem, a bad attitude and a poor mentality. See how ridiculous that sounds? Oh please! Spare me the nonsense already. For heaven's sake already,don't believe the hype. Ladies, don't you dare fall for those lies. Experiences don't make you, they help to evolve you. Therefore, any bad experience you have had girlfriend let it go, don't dwell and FORGET ABOUT IT. Why let things of the past control your now and your future. You won't get anywhere if you are still dwelling on things of the pasts. The past is the past for a reason. Appreciate those experiences for what they taught you. Accept them fully, understand that they have made you the strong person you are, and then move forward with your life.

Release the trash . . . .

Have you ever heard the term spring cleaning? Well, if you haven't it is a phrase that refers to eliminating and getting rid of anything unnecessary, useless, a waste of time, efforts, and space. However, for the purposes of the "release the trash lesson" we are focusing on releasing the negative, toxic, and critical people that may be in your life. I actually think that this "spring cleaning" term needs to apply all year around, for every season. Spring cleaning is no easy task, I will tell you that. You have to pull things, push things, pack up, box up, clean behind, pick up, rearrange, sort, and move. I mean it takes some energy to do. This is why people procrastinate. They don't feel like going through the hassle. "I'll do it another day." No, do it today! Today is cleanup day. Do you have on your clean up gear? We will start at the front and work our way to the back, okay? There is a method to this, sure there is. Absolutely! What do you want to tackle first? Let's tackle immediate family. What do you mean, Ms. Davis? I got to wipe out my family? Unfortunately, yes! If there are negative people in your family that are causing you stress, and bringing you down, you have to get rid of them. You don't need that type of energy around you on your new path of love, positive thinking, success and happiness. Positivity and negativity don't mix, sorry to break it down like that. But it is the truth. If you want positive things to happen in your life, you have to put yourself in positive situations, and around positive people. I don't care who you have to release, whether it be your mother, father, brother, sister, aunt, cousins, uncles, grandparents, significant other, it does not matter.

If there is anyone in your life who is talking negative to you, belittling you, downing your dreams, discouraging you, or has no belief and faith in you, remove them from your life. Do not give pre-warning, ultimatum, or pleading, give them the boot, kick to the curb. We talked about kicking the negative thoughts out, the same thing goes for those negative people. They too must go. Like a garage sale, "EVERYTHING MUST GO." Give it to somebody else who wants it, the negativity, and drama, because we in the hell sure don't need it, and will not be using it. We are gladly releasing negativity, and are giving it away freely. Put up a big ass sign marked FREE NEGATIVITY GIVEAWAYS. Watch and see how that draws some attention. LOL, Slap high five on that one! You are feeling me, aren't you girl? Yes, I'm so serious.

Ladies, as if we do not have enough to be concerned about with trying to follow our dreams and obtain our goals, the last thing we need is to be surrounding by negative people. Aint nobody got time for that! It is those same negative dream killers who aren't doing a damn thing with their lives. Mad at you because you actually want something in life, and instead of being there to support you, they would rather rain on your parade. What a shame! But, you aren't going to let them though, I am confident of that. This is why, we got to get this trash out of your life, Immediately! Trash pickup is today.

You grab that, and I will grab this. I'm helping you walk the trash out, and setting it by the back door. I am sure you won't miss that (dusting hands off).

Recap, so we *got that covered.* We called for backup, our support system, check! Got out of our own way with the negative thoughts, check! Forgot about the past and the things holding us back, check! And released the trash, toxic people, and check! Yup, I'll say we covered it all. Everything seems to be falling into place, my friend. That is exactly how we want it. There are a few more things we need to do that will help us in our mission. Lesson five *finally out of the box*, will focus on expanding our horizons and our new outlook on life. Followed by lesson six, *it's a mind thing,* where we will talk about positive thinking and changing thoughts. Last, we will wrap up our lessons with some playback exercises. Aren't you excited? I saved the best for last. Stay with me, we're going to really have fun.

 *Lesson five*

Finally out of the box

Girlfriend, we were throwing away trash in the last lesson, and there were some things that we left out of the box. But don't panic! These are actually useful. As there were a lot of things we did not need and were discarded, we made sure to set aside the things that we do need. One of the things that we decided to keep is our new outlook on life.

This new outlook involves seeing the beauty in everything we once had. There was beauty in not knowing ourselves at a point in time. Beauty can be found in the fact that we had to find ourselves in the process. It was beautiful that we had to do self-assessing, evaluating and improvements. There was beauty to be found was in not knowing our way, and having to understand our purpose in life. There was beauty in the pain, the confusion, the disappointment, and the rejections. There was beauty in those negative, toxic and critical people that were once in our lives. It all can be seen as once beautiful.

Sounds crazy? Ok, let me explain. If you did not have those experiences, how would you know any better? How would you want what you never had? How would you recognize good when you saw it? How would you want to change? Do you think that you would be where you are now? Good questions, don't you think? I would say so. We got what we needed out of those thing. Now they are used up, worn out and are no longer needed. And that's exactly how we want it. So, it is time for a change. I think we should do something different. Do you have any idea what you would like to try next? Think about it? It's time we try something new.

Expand your horizons . . .

What we needed to keep is your new open mind. Anything telling you what you shouldn't do please leave that in the closed BOX. What closed box? You know the one with the four corners, four walls, four flaps, that easily press down, fold, and attach. Easy instructions, right? Yup, boxes are simple. There ain't nothing complicated or interesting about a box. On the other hand, this new outlook and open mind should expand our horizons. Out with the old and in with the new. New life, new thoughts, new friends, new support, new opportunities, new beginnings, and new you.

Sound great, right? But in order to do this, we should first focus on reinventing and recreating ourselves. It's MAKEOVER time. YAY!!! A girls favorite thing to do. I am talking about the works girl. They say beauty hurts, but not in this case. It's going to feel GREAT!!! We will do things we've never done before. We will go places we've never gone before. We will talk to people we've never talked to before. We will think as we never thought before. We will act as we've never acted before. We will speak as we've never spoken before. Everything will be new and different. You get the drift? I know all about "expanding your horizons." Details, you want? Of course, I got you! I have one word for you EXPLORE!

Care to elaborate, Ms. Davis? (Shrugs shoulders). You know I will, just wanted to make sure I had your attention. I encourage you to step outside of your normal is what I mean by that. Get out of your comfort zone and try new things. It was like I started to see the world in a different light when I finally got out of my comfort zone and expanded my horizons. Everything seemed to be different to me. I then wondered what I had been doing all that time before. Was I sleep walking? Or Was I daydreaming? Who knows? All I knew was when I finally opened my eyes and looked, I loved what I saw. I was able to live the life I wanted, finally. Explore, be free, and be me. I was ready to be explore life with my new confidence and outlook. I was strutting my stuff and feeling good doing it. Sashay, sashay, happy twirl and a spin. Look at me y'all, all eyes on me. It was nothing to stop me. I was fierce, fly and unstoppable.

I was ready to take on the world. That is what a new look will do to you. It make me feel like I could conquer the world. And so I did, and I am. Would you like to feel this way too? I amsure you would. Trust me, this new look will do you some good. You are going to feel like a new woman, I promise you? Do you trust me? I can go get the makeup kit and help to transform you, if you like. This new thing that we are going to try is completely OUT OF THE BOX. Hope you are ready for this. How's about it? I am on my way to get that new life, are you coming too?

How to expand your horizons . . . .

There are no step by step instructions on how to do this. This part is on you. There are so many ways to expand your horizons but I will share a few. College! OMG (oh my goodness), what is she talking about now? I am saying miss missy that College is one way we can expand our horizons. How, you ask? What does College have to do with one's "horizons?" As a matter of fact, it has a lot to do with it. Grab your pen and paper get ready to take notes. Don't want you to miss out on any important information. Class is in session. Are you ready to learn? It was actually College that help trained my THOUGHTS. I mean, I learned how to actually think for myself. Imagine that! I had a brain but didn't know how to use it.Crazy huh? Well, it is true.

Before attending college, I was use to my own naive way of thinking, my own little philosophies and little small mind which had a hard time comprehending and conceptualizing complex concepts. It was in College, I learned how to apply critical thinking to my life. Being required to analyze situations and produce solutions was not something I was forced to do in "real life." This taught me how to thoroughly think through problems to come up with solutions.

In addition, it allowed me to handle challenging ideas and difficulties. Studying, reading and learning created mental stimulation as something that was lacking in evident of my activities. This was an outlet and substitution from being mentally corrupted by watching pointless stuff on television. It gave me something to do, and got my mind out of dumb mode, for a lack of better words. However, College is not easy. Not at all Sorry, I am being honest. It just isn't. But it will challenge you. Challenged I was indeed. I appreciated, and needed the learning experience. I mostly appreciate some of the people I met both classmates and professors.

One particular person, I will never forget is Professor Ivy Cobbins (Olive-Harvey College). Now she put the C in Challenge. She was demanding. The expectations of her courses really made me learn the value of thinking. Aside from being a rough teacher, this lady is so wise. I use to sit in her class and just soak up all her knowledge and wisdom. I would simply be in awe when she spoke. The way she would say things really made the wheels in my head turn. Talk about thought-provoking. She made me think about and analyze everything. Other students thought she was mean and tough, but I thought she was refreshing. I believe she was tough on her students, especially those she saw potential in. I adore that woman. I had to give a quick shout out to Dr. Cobbins, and say thank you. Back to business. Expanding your horizons!

Well, I was saying girlfriend. Sometimes you won't know what you like until you try it. While, I understand that College is not for everyone, it was merely a suggestion. There are plenty of new things that you can do to explore. How about activities? They are a great way to find your passions and discover the possibilities. Zip lining, mountain climbing, Opera, ballet, painting, and even pole dancing are great activities. This sounds like fun, doesn't it? I have engaged in them all. Really, Opera? Yes OPERaaaaa (singing). This was an indescribable experience. I was out of my element for sure. Never in my wildest dreams, did I think that I would sit in an Opera theater. Besides, I am a black woman. Black women don't go to the Opera, they say. Well, this one did, and she loved it. For so long I lived in a little box. I lived in my little mind, in my little community, and in my little circle. I had refused to be different and explore because I needed people to accept me, especially my own "people." I did not want to be called a freak or weirdo so this prevented me from doing all that I desired to do. Again, I conformed to those opinions, stigmas, and expectation of society. One should stick to what one knows right? Wrong! I don't want to stick to what I know, what fun is that? I want to be different. I like to explore. I like to take chances, and I like to go with the flow.

What's the lessons here? The lesson is forget about what you are used to. Forget the boredom, mundane, average, and routine and mediocrity. Forget about fitting in with the crowd. Forget about being like everyone else. Forget about what everyone else says you should and shouldn't do. How can people tell you what to do? Doesn't everyone else do what they want to do? Well, why can't you t too? Who gives a damn? This is your life. You have the right to do whatever the hell you want to do, when you feel like doing it, and how you feel like doing it. There I go again, throwing away the directions, and just going with the flow. Yes, I will admit, I tend to do that from time to time. That's me, queen of randomness, princess of adventure, and lady of spontaneity. But, don't just love that about me? LOL. I feel everyone should have a bit of random in them. Being risky, good risky, helps to get out the box and expand your horizons. How did I become this way? I wasn't always this way. I said to myself one day, "girl have fun, live, learn, experience and enjoy. SHE'S BEYOND THOSE THOUGHTS that life is all about pain, struggle, misery and BOREDOM. I know you are thinking to yourself that I say that boredom word a lot, and you are right I do. It is the one thing I dislike. Boredom drives me LOCO. I can't express that enough. We should live a life of excitement, enjoyment and thrills.

Let us live a life we would be proud of. Life is what we make it. Those are the thoughts that you need to wake up with each and every day. Say to yourself "I will make the best out of this life because I only have one life to live." This is our new motto, okay ladies? It is not difficult to do. I know it isn't. You aced this lesson. You are a great student. Wrapping it up, as we are working on expanding our horizons, it is very important to make valuable connections. People learn from other people, that's the order of this learning thing. In the next lesson we will talk about networking and meeting new people.

Pleasure to make your acquaintance . . .

Sometimes it is not what you know, but who you know. This is important as it pertains to success. If you want to get ahead in life, network and meet new people. It can help get you to the next level. The people we meet can help us make it in this world. People make the world go around, they say. I will have to agree with this. No one is in this world alone. We are a collective body of beings having what is known as a human experience. Without people there would not be a "world." In this world we form connections with one another. It is the connections with one another that form this collective body of people. There goes Ms. Philosopher again? Why yes I am! Stop rolling your eyes, and don't you dare walk away. You may want to stick around for this. How does meeting and connecting with people help to broaden my perspectives and horizons? It does in more ways than one. Would you like me to continue? Okay, certainly!

It is a simple fact of life that people influence our lives. Point, blank, and period! I am attempting to impact yours through this book and conversation, in a positive way, of course. The good news is while people influence us, we, believe it or not have the control of who we let affect our lives. If negative people can have an effect on us, so can positive people. It goes both ways. In this lesson, we will talk about the positive people we need to add to our lives. Wine? Oh yeah, I almost forgot about that. No thanks, I think I will have to pass, am at my limit but you go ahead and help yourself. I don't mind if you do.

Hello, hi, how are you doing? Shake hands. My name is Tameisha Davis, and what yours? Pleasure to make your acquaintance. See, it's not hard to introduce ourselves to new people. There's nothing to it but to do it. It is very easy to do. However, the thing that stops us from introducing ourselves to new people, environment, and situations is F. E. A. R, Forces, Encouraging, Aggressive, Resistance. As I mentioned before being afraid of what people think of us, how they view us, trying to impress, trying to attract, trying to fit in, and trying to be accepted are the things that hold us back in many interactions and situations. We can longer have these thoughts because we are beyond those thoughts, remember? We said we wanted a new life and meeting new people comes with that territory.Our focus now is meeting POSITIVE people that who add value to our lives. Nice people! Kind people! Understanding people! Compassionate people! Caring People! Loving people! Fun people! Happy people! People person people! Widen your circle to these type of people. Expand, increase and stretch the limited spaces of your life. It's good to let people in. Not everyone comes to steal your joy. Send out a personal invitation to POSITIVE people to join your life's party. No RSVP needed, and they don't have to bring anything but a positive spirit. Treat positive people like an open door policy, all are welcomed and walk-ins are accepted.

Too often, we're afraid let people in and open the doors because we are afraid they will take advantage, use, abuse, and mistreat us. We have our guards up to protect ourselves so we are not mistreated. I am not telling you to put your guard down but you can lower it a tad bit, low enough to see what the person is all about. Give positivity a chance, come on now. Remember your mother told you never to talk to strangers? Sorry to say, momma was wrong. These are not strangers, these are our new friends. These are not those bad guys she warned us about. They are good people. These people would not hurt us. They want to help us. Positive people are looking to help. We positive people, yes, I am including myself want to see everyone prosper, and are dedicated to lifting other's spirits. Positive plus positive equals positive, something I love to quote. The thing I am trying to express is that when you surround yourself with positive people it will rub off on you. You will find yourself being a more positive person as a result. I hope all this makes sense my dearest friend. Positive people in, negative people out, enough said. Shall we move on? The next lesson is "It's a mind thing." Get ready to be enlightened.

Lesson six

It's a MIND thing

I believe that all things first originate in the mind. Feelings, ideas, THOUGHTS, relationships, success, failure, love, and happiness. It all develops from our minds. How can this be you ask? Doesn't the heart play a role too? Yes, it does. But like the rock, paper, scissors game the mind beats the heart. How can the mind beat the heart when they are interconnected? I understand one can't survive without the other, and the heart is just as powerful as the mind? This is true. I meant the mind beats the heart in a metaphorical sense. For example, people always say, "follow your heart" or "let your heart lead you." While I knowingly receive this concept, I do not completely agree. My philosophy is quite the opposite. I feel that we should lead with our minds.

How does one know what's in one's heart, if they haven't first conjured the idea? How does one know what one feels, if they haven't first thought about it? How does one know what one believes, if they haven't imagined it? Do you see where I am coming from? These things come from our brain, IT'S A MIND THING. In this lesson, we are challenging all of these things (feelings, ideas, negativity, etc.) with the power of positive thinking. Hey, wake up! I know you aren't nodding off to sleep. Don't you dare fall asleep! We have come to the best part. This is the part you have been waiting for. We are going to learn how to think POSITIVE, change our THOUGHTS and be SUCCESSFUL.

Mind Power . . . .

Have you ever heard of the Jedi Mind Trick? No! Well, this is when you have the ability to persuade and influence someone to do something you want them to do using the power of the mind. I got this concept from the movie "Star Wars." Stop laughing at me. I am not crazy, lol. I got a brilliant idea. Please hear me out! Ok, I was thinking how about we apply this notion to our way of thinking. Ladies, lets use the Jedi Mind trick on our own mind using the POSITIVE thinking technique. We will be able to get our minds to do what we want it to do. Genius, Right? We should try this, it may work. Using the POSITIVE THINKING technique we will get our minds to think good thoughts, self-improvement thoughts, self-love thoughts, thoughts of success, thoughts of dreams and aspirations achieved, caring thoughts, and positive thoughts.

Unlike Stars Wars, there is no magic or special wand involved. There is no secret weapon or trick to make positive thoughts appear. The only secret weapon we are using here to combat those negative forces is our positive thinking. Grab your positive thinking weapon and break it down so that you can clearly understand. Mind Power, we we're talking about mind power, right? Okay, I was saying that our mind is the most powerful thing we have in this world and "with great power comes great responsibility "~Stan Lee. We can use our mind for ultimate power. Many people don't really understand this concept. However, great minds do.

Because the mind is the most powerful thing we have, it can be used for good or bad. Let's use our MIND POWER for the greater good. It is easy to choose to use it for bad. But how easy is it to use for good? There is enough bad and negative minds in the world today. We don't need you to add to it with your negative thoughts? Let's not do that! We need a more positive world. We can bring that element of positive energy, positive thoughts and a positive life. Ms. Davis, you talk so confidently about this positive stuff. Why is that? Let me express that, I am now a firm believer in the power of positive thinking, and the amazing things it has done in my life. How is that, you ask? Girl, I use to be one negative ass person. I am talking critically negativveeee. I always had something negative to say about everything and everyone. I used to THINK negative about everything and everyone. I had a hard time seeing the positive and beauty in things. I used my past experiences and pain to fuel those negative thoughts.

Negativity didn't do anything but spark fires. It poured gasoline on family and friends, and struck the match. Poof!!!! The negativity went up in big flames. Negativity caused great damaged and wreaked havoc on everything in my life. I suffered inside, and the negative was sure to bring it out. It convinced me that I was broken, and had some internal mess going on inside of me. It told me to take my anger, and bitterness out on everything, and everyone. Besides, what did I have to be positive for, I thought? Negativity had somehow deluded my mind into believing that life had dealt me a bad hand. I was duped, hoodwinked, and bamboozled by that pesky negativity. It was a slick little sucker. It got me good. All this negativity did was cause more problems in my life.

And what did all this negativity get me? Nothing. What did I benefit? Nothing. What did I gain? You guessed it, nothing. Listen to me when I tell you. It doesn't do anything but push people away. When this happens you are left with your negative mind, negative thoughts, and negative life. How can you progress and be successful with this negativity? You can't. How can you be happy with negativity? You can't. How can you enjoy life with negativity? Once again, you can't. Whoa, this is my confession (in my Usher voice). Not only was I negative about people, but I had negative self-esteem. I felt negative about myself. "I am not pretty enough. I am not smart enough. I am not good enough." I constantly fed my mind with these negative thoughts, every day. You know how some people wake up in the morning and have their morning cup of coffee? Me, I woke up every day to the daily dose of negativity. Sad woman, as I look back on that and shake my head. But it's okay. That's why we have new days. This is where change comes in.

Do you want a different life? If so, to have a different life, change the way you think. Yes, change your thoughts! It's that simple. This is what I have done. Nowadays, people don't know what the hell is wrong with me. I am so positive. I mean, I stay POSITIVE, think POSITIVE, and live POSITIVE. I am constantly talking about being positive. Yes, ME! So, all the days of waking up with a negative attitude are far behind me. What a sigh of relief and burden lifted off of me. Now, it is your turn, to be relieved. Time to work on you as we will learn how to disable and disengage those negative thoughts.

How to control negative thoughts . . . .

I will make these steps as simple as possible. Easy as 1, 2, 3. We will start with Step 1. Develop a strong mind. I'll further explain, but let me catch my breath. Okay, I'm ready! First things first negative thoughts are detrimental to your mental health. One way we can control negative thoughts is by developing a healthy relationship with positive thoughts. Healthiness involves strength. We need a strong mind. In other words be strong-minded. One must have a great deal of willpower. Strong minded individuals are not easily influenced, and have an independent way of thinking. When you have a strong mind, you can control the negative thoughts. You control the access that negativity has to your brain. It is determined by you when they enter, and when they leave. Didn't know you could, do that huh? Well, you can. A strong mind will allow you to recognize and pick up on the signals when negativity is attempting to enter your brain. To develop a strong-mind, we will learn how to rewire our brains, (thinking).We need to take the negative lines, switch them, and cross over to connect to the positive ones. No research on this, just another brilliant metaphor, lol. Compare positive thinking to starting a stalled car. Those of us with *hoopties* (raggedy cars) know all about giving *a jump*. Apply this concept to negative verses positive thinking. Negative thoughts stall us and to get going again let us use positive thoughts to gives us a jump start. Clever, right? Oh that Tameisha, lol. I.K.R (I know, right). I told you it would make sense. Changing our thinking process is the only way we will master positive thinking. Stay focused only on positive things, and watch your mind transform. Are you ready to move on to step two, now?

Step two, in controlling the negative thoughts, it is good to utilize positive affirmations, mantras and quotes. We briefly discussed this in lesson two. I want to talk a little more about the importance of affirmations because this is how you actually start to think positive. Positive affirmations and mantras are a great way to help you get you into the habit of speaking positive words to yourself. You will practically be convincing your mind to think good thoughts. Spoken affirmations involve you having a personal conversation with yourself. However, you aren't seeking answers. In this conversation you are talking to you, and you are doing both the listening and responding. You may feel weird doing this, at first. Trust me, this is perfectly normal. You are not crazy because you are talking to yourself. Yeah, whatever you say? And this is coming from the crazy lady? I feel you! I assure you that this will work, you can take my word for it. We previously went over some affirmations that you can say to yourself. Let's repeat those now. Repeat after me "I am smart. I am intelligent. I am beautiful. I am creative. I am loving. I am unique. I am special. I am amazing." Please repeat one more time. Thank you! I want you to remember that repetition in spoken affirmations is most effective. These sort of words do great at improving our self-esteem. The goal is for us to feel better about ourselves. This will improve our way of thinking as a result. Do you want to try a few more, since we are on a role? Okay, here we. Repeat these words "I am happy. I am great. I am good." Again, "I am happy. I am great. I am good." Yup, I think you got it. I can see you improving already. I need you to do me a favor. Will you promise me that you will speak affirmations to yourself every day? Will you do that? Please!

Positive quotes are good at creating positive thoughts as well. Reading positive quotes are effective in removing negative thoughts from the mind. My favorite quote is "Be the change you wish to see in this world"~ Gandhi. I quote this every day. This particular quote is useful if you are trying to change any old habits. I have the Gandhi quote posted on my bedroom wall above my bed. I read it aloud every day as it keeps me focused. You can find all sorts of quotes that relate to what you are going through, or want to change. As I said before, it all just depends on where you are in your life. You can easily find quotes that reflect your interest. A good idea is to try browsing the internet for some positive quotes. You can also purchase books on the subject of positive affirmations and quotes. Whether you get them from the internet or a book, makes no difference. The important thing is to make affirmations, quotes and mantras a part of your daily ritual. Okay, I think that about sums it up. Would you like to continue or do you need another wine break, lol?

Positively easy . . . .

A lot of times we make things more complicated than they have to be. Why make things difficult if they do not have to be? In this lesson I would like to suggest 5 easy and practical things that you can do to think to stay positive. Practice these on a daily basis as they will increase your level of positive thoughts.

1. Say Cheese

You want to think positive? SMILE. Wow, that's it? Yup! That's it. Smile more. CHEESE, let me see those pearly whites. Smiling helps to improve your mood and increase positive thoughts. This is something that always seem to put me in a good mood. And the best part is, you don't have to be smiling at anything in particular. Just simply smile for damn reason, lol. Plus, it will do your face some good. It can also keep you looking youthful. It will help to block those lines and wrinkles too. Ladies, and we all want to look young, right? Well you better start smiling. "A smile," the ultimate wrinkle cream, title of my next book, lol. If you want to be positive just "put on a happy face."

2. Soothe my soul

Music is good for the soul. Listening to smooth, inspirational music also put me in a good mood and improve positive thoughts. I like classical, Jazz, Opera, and symphony. All of these genres of music stimulate the mind and create the flow of positive thoughts. If you don't like the instrumental type of music. R&B, Country and some Hip Hop is fine. It all just depends on the message that they send. Let's try to steer clear of hard core or negative music that send wrong messages. This does no good for creating positive thoughts. Our goal is INSPIRATION, and UPLIFTING, which ultimately helps lead to positive thoughts. Good music always uplifts the spirit.

3. Get Busy

Can you say productivity? Productive people are usually positive people. When you occupy your time with productive activities, you really have no time to be negative. It is easy to get in a negative mood and mind frame when you have nothing to do. Activity preoccupies your brain and mind which gives less attention to entertaining negative thoughts. It can be the simplest activities such as cooking, cleaning, shopping, reading, and crafting that can give your mind some busy work to do. When I get a negative thought mood, I immediately engage myself in some kind of mental or physical activity. I do all of the above. They work great too.I almost forgot to tell you, EXERCISE! Exercise is also a great way to improve your mood and increase positive thoughts. It doesn't require a gym membership or fancy equipment. Walk! If is nice outdoors, go for a walk. Let the fresh air and scenery uplift your spirits, and ease negative thoughts. I love to take long walks in the park. The trees, the smell of grass, nature, are all inspiring and motivational. If you do not have the opportunity to walk outdoor, try exercising indoors. This works as well. Are you keeping track of all this information? I am giving you good stuff here, lol.

4. Lend a hand

I don't know about you but I feel good about myself when I can help someone else. Extending a helping hand can also help to create positive thoughts. As we discussed before we are collective body of human beings having a human experience and depend on each other for daily survival. What did I just say? Let me rephrase that in laymen's terms, we all are people on this earth together. We can help each other. I believe this is what life is all about. Helping one another. Engaging in charitable and humanitarian efforts are great at improving positive thoughts. LEND ME A HAND would you please? I will be happy to lend you mine. By the way, you owe me remember? I helped you take out that trash a few lessons ago. You thought I forgot about that, didn't you. No, I didn't. Now, it's time to return the favor, pay up, lol.

5. *Lighten up*

Life is hard enough, why add more stress and pressure by coming down on yourself? We tend to do this to ourselves often, and for what reasons ladies? I know about this firsthand. I use to be my own worst enemy. I used to be obsessed with trying to be Ms. Perfect. What is have found interesting was that these perfectionist tendencies seemed to creative even more negative self-thoughts. A perfectionist to a fault. Stop the pick, pick, and picking at yourself. Stop dissecting yourself to the core. Ok, this is wrong. The only thing this dissection does is target all the negative flaws and imperfections. When you are done picking yourself apart you are left with a long list of "fix me ups." Yes, everyone should improve, but who want a long list of things wrong. Let's focus on one thing at a time. This list just creates negative thoughts. My advice to you is STOP beating up on yourself. No one is perfect. When we realize this, we won't doubt our abilities as often. We will develop more faith, and have a loving attitude toward ourselves. Lastly, stop stressing over not being where you want to be in life or doing what you would like to be doing. As long as you are giving things your best efforts, then you should be happy. Know that you are doing well. You are trying to be the best you. Keep focusing only on the good and this will create positive thoughts. Do I make myself clear? Just playing, ladies. Keep those thoughts positive and everything will be good. OKAY?

Wrap Up Lesson . . . .

Ladies, I hate to end our session but we are out of time and wine, lol. That wraps of this episode of SHE'S BEYOND THOSE

THOUGHTS. This has been an enlightening conversation my friend, I feel so much better. How about you? I appreciate your valuable time and you being brave enough to open up with me. I really enjoyed talking to you. With that said, I hope you are encourage to go after the life that you want with your mind filled with POSITIVE THOUGHTS. But before, I go I will leave you with a few PLAYBACK EXERCISES. These will aid you in the lessons we covered. Practice these as they are helpful. And until we meet again. STAY POSITIVE . . . . BLESSINGS!

PLAYBACK EXERCISES

Lesson one: Defining that defining moment, EXERCISE
Calming Ritual

When going through the defining moment process sometimes it's just best to do absolutely nothing. Relax your mind. Spend quiet time alone. Just chill, and relax because sometimes the mind just needs a break.

Instructions

1. Find a quiet area or designated spot. Let's create a calming ambiance. Bedrooms and bathrooms are ideal for this activity. We need someplace serene and inviting for tranquility.

2. Preferably a dim lighted area will work. Illuminate area with lamps or candles. I like to use red lights. RED LIGHT SPECIAL!

3. Ignite the senses. Scented candles and incense are great for this. It is the aroma that helps to sooth and calm your mind

and nerves. Lavender, vanilla and ginger scents are good to use.

4. Lay back, relax, and breathe deeply. This also helps to ease nerves and tension. Ahhhh . . . Breath in, breath out!

5. Play music. Soothing music. Jazz, classical and symphony is also calming and will help to relax your mind. Let the music set you free.

6. If you choose the bathroom as your calming ambiance, take a warm bath with bubbles, lavender or chamomile scent. (Recommended).

7. And don't forget the WINE, whichever you prefer. I like red wine.

8. Now feel cool, calm and relaxed . . . . CHILL

Lesson two: Finding you in the process, EXERCISE

Self-Assessment

If you want to do something that requires deep contemplating, reflecting and thinking about who you are. Written exercises are great tools. This will require the use of writing, so you will actually need a pen for this. You can write your ideas here in this guide. There is plenty of space to do that.

Who am I, characteristics (good ones) let's list them here. Try to think of at least 15 positive traits.

1.   9.

2.   10.

3.   11.

4.   12.

5.   13.

6.   14.

7.   15.

8.

After you are done with this exercise. FOCUS on these POSITIVE characteristics.

If you have to look at this list every day to remind yourself of the positive characteristic, feel free to do so.

Lesson Three: A passion for passion, EXERCISE

Activities & Likes

Sometimes it can be difficult to identify our passions, mainly because we are not sure what we like to do or are good at. Again, written exercise help to obtain clarity. In this exercise please think for a moment what you like to do. I mean really love doing. It doesn't matter what it is. I want you to make a list of 10 things you enjoy doing and are passionate about.

I am passionate about and like to do . . . .

1.   6.

2.   7.

3.   8.

4.   9.

5.   10.

Use this list as encouragement and a reminder to do more of what you love every chance you get. Let your passions lead you in your daily activities. Remember to keep your passions alive.

Lesson four: Got that covered EXERCISE

Progress & forward movement

In order for us to progress in life, we need to be able to recognize all the things that hold us back. In this exercise reach out to a friend or family you know to discuss some things that may be holding you back. Sometimes we can't recognize our own faults, and so it's good to get an objective opinion from our friends and family whom come to know us personally. Ask them what they think are some things that may be holding you back in life. It is just their opinion, but take it as constructive criticism. Only seek out those people who have your best interest at heart.

From that conversation write down at least 10 of those things that you think may be holding you back from your fullest potential. List them here. Use this list to make self-improvement and changes in your life.

I will no longer let . . . . hold me back!

1.   6.

2.   7.

3.   8.

4.   9.

5.   10.

Lesson Five: Finally out of the box, EXERCISE

Actions required

Written exercises are my favorite, as you can see. You will soon come to like them too. In this exercise we will write down goals, dreams, activities, etc., that will require immediate action. The sooner you do these, the sooner you will start to see results in your life. Positive results. I want you to write down 12 things that you would like to do, but have yet had the opportunity. I chose the number 12 since there are twelve months in a year. Try to do at least 1 new thing each month over the course of a year. Look at this as your bucket list. It could be places you would like to go. Things you would like to see. People you want to talk to. Anything. This exercise will required ACTION.

I would like to experience . . . .

1.   7.

2.   8.

3.   9.

4.   10.

5.   11.

6.   12.

Lesson six: It's a mind thing, EXERCISE

Self-Affirmation

As we discussed in *it's a mind thing* lesson, affirmations are important in constant positive thinking. In this exercise you will need a mirror. Doesn't matter what size as long as you are able to see your face in it. Sounds interesting? Yes, it is. We will use the mirror for self-talk and affirmations. Did you find a mirror? Hell, used a spoon if you have to, as long as you can see yourself. Take your reflecting object, put it up to your face, so you can get a good look, and I want you to repeat these words.

Say aloud . . . 2x each
I am pretty sexy
I am fine as can be
I am as cute as a button
I am beautiful made
I am so gorgeous
I like what I see
I love my eyes
I have a pretty smile
I love my nose
I love my completion
I am really unique
I am very special
I am too amazing
I am so damn wonderful

Ladies, remember this and tell yourself these words every time you look into a mirror. Give yourself compliments, don't wait for others to. Look good and feel good. This will help you to be positive.

 About The Author

I was born, raised and currently reside in Chicago, Illinois. I attended and graduated from Paul Robeson H.S. located on the Southside of Chicago. In education pursuits, excellence is something I have always strived for. From my childhood and early beginnings, I always dreamed of becoming a writer. Writing was something that always came naturally to me as a form of expression. Therefore, this experience has really become a dream come true. Throughout my life I've had a deep passion for learning as well. However, it wasn't until I grew older that I actually decided to take it seriously and attend college. In 2010 at age 30, I received an Associate's degree at Olive-Harvey College. Thereafter, wanting to continue my education I went to DeVry University where I obtained a Bachelor's degree in human resource-technical management. Today, I am still actively engaged in educational pursuits and am studying for a Master's degree in human resource management at Keller Graduate School of Management. My ultimate goal is to earn a Ph.D. in educational psychology, and inspire other women & mothers to accomplish their goals, follow their dreams and acquire a successful life filled POSITIVE THOUGHTS . . . .